Peaceful Pondering

Peaceful Pondering

A Busy Woman's Guide to Inner Peace

Teri Coaxum

Rev. date: 05/30/2017

To order additional copies of this book, contact:
Xlibris
1-888-795-4274
www.Xlibris.com
Orders@Xlibris.com
761088

Peaceful Pondering – A Busy Woman's Guide to Inner Peace

I pray that this book will assist you in finding inner peace so that you can realize the joy that is life. You're worth it. Are you tired, frustrated, lack motivation, feeling depleted and unsuccessful? This quick guide will help you identify the cause and show you how to stay sane by finding balance and peace.

Contents

Foreword

In our busy lives, it is easy to lose sight of what is truly important. As women, we tend to forget that taking care of ourselves is not "selfish" but instead translates into better taking care of our families and more positively impacting our communities.

I have known Teri Coaxum for 15+ years and I have witnessed her make a real difference in politics, policy and community service. She is someone who is wholly committed to doing what is right and someone who always puts forth her best not only in her work but also in her relationships. Her formidable spirit, tenacity, and savvy are an inspiration for women in general, and young women and girls in particular.

Teri has mastered the art and science of burning the candle at both ends, so it makes perfect sense that she has allowed her voice and her story to be included among the collective leadership experience of professional women, and shared a useful formula to help women take on all of life's challenges and still be at peace.

Teri has had many successes in her professional life, receiving numerous awards from government, academic, philanthropic and community sectors. She accepts these accolades not for work accomplished, but as a reminder of the goals to which she's committed.

Thus, she continues to be an agent of change, infusing her experience and passion to forge strategic alliances to advance human, social and economic development.

She continues to excel and stay centered, guided by the lessons taught by the many powerful women upon whose shoulders we stand, and committed to helping women focus on their enormous untapped potential.

This small but powerful guide to inner peace comes to you from the mind and heart of a skilled communicator, a bold and confident leader and an exceptional human being. She is a strong, kind and multi-talented woman.

I hope this guide helps you draw from Teri's passion and insight as you forge your own path to inner peace, and that it helps you to remember to always be kind and take care of yourself.

Yvonne J. Graham
Associate Commissioner
Director, Office of Minority Health & Health Disparities Prevention
New York State Department of Health

Introduction

In this world of facebook, twitter, instagram, snapchat, periscope, live streaming, cellphones, tablets, and desktops, we don't have an "off" button. We often find ourselves juggling many tasks at once. Because of this, we are heading toward burnout with no way to stop a head-on collision. This book will offer some quick tools to sustain you so you can be successful. I understand what you are facing. You're not alone. Life gets in the way. I once read in *Meditation in a New York Minute* by Mark Thornton, "Deep inside of us now lies a space that is always calm." It is extremely important that you find that calm. I challenge you to find it not by seeking balance but learning to integrate the important things in your life. Understand first that not everything can be a priority. Also understand that something will come along and be more pressing than something else. Something will require your immediate attention. By integrating, you take away the stress of always trying to find balance because you know different situations will tip the scales of balance. Integration will allow you to "have it all," stress free. In this book we'll define and discover peace, your peace. We'll discover the calm that's deep inside each and every one of us when we silence the constant chatter.

Chapter 1

Are You Ready For a Paradigm Shift?

"Peace of mind is not the absence of conflict from life,
but the ability to cope with it."

~ Unknown

In our hyper-connected digital-overload world, we don't have an "off" button. We spend our days checking our email, scrolling through our facebook newsfeed and live-tweeting everything from how we feel to what we had for lunch. We are not even sure ourselves what we are hoping to achieve by over-sharing, but we do know that staying "logged on" makes us feel like we've got our finger on the pulse. To be logged off is to be shut out. Getting views and likes from strangers or acquaintances fills us with a sense of worthiness, albeit fleeting. Our mood can be sent spiraling downward with even the slightest hint of negativity. We toggle from task to task, never really focused but always busy. We spread ourselves too thin and take on too many responsibilities, all the while wishing our lives were as flawless as a Pinterest pin, but knowing we'll never quite get there. The end result of this 21st century lifestyle is a kind of frenzy that will inevitably lead to burn out, depression, panic, self-loathing and many other destructive emotions that complete the toxic picture.

But it doesn't have to be this way. You can stop this vicious cycle of information overload in a hamster wheel existence. I wrote this guide to offer some quick tools to inspire and sustain you so you can be successful, happy and at peace with yourself. You can create a paradigm shift in your life. You can get rid of old habits that no longer serve you and create new habits. You can access that quiet sacred space inside you that you know exists, where everything is just as it should be and you are at peace.

I've been where you are today. I know how easy it is to fall into the trap of doing too much and achieving in the worldly sense, but at the same time losing myself. I am busy professional, a nurturing mom and grandmother, a business advocate, business owner, life coach, author, community leader, motivational speaker, mentor, and professor (both undergraduate and graduate). I lived a stressed-out existence for many years!

I'm here to tell you that it is extremely important that you find that calm space within yourself. I challenge you to find it not by seeking balance but by learning to integrate the important things in your life. By removing the added stress of seeking a balance that can never exist, you can focus on integration. Not everything can be a priority. And priorities shift. Something more pressing will come along while you're trying to prioritize and your immediate attention will be required.

That's ok. In this guide I will teach you ways to set your priorities and keep them through integration, while maintaining the flexibility required in our modern world. In this book we will define and discover your peace. We will seek out and find the calm that's deep inside of each of us when we silence the constant chatter that threatens to rob us of our chance at lasting happiness.

I'm so glad you decided to join me on this journey toward inner peace. I know what you're going through and I know I can help you. ***Now onward! Take Action!***

Chapter 2

What Exactly is Inner Peace?

"The life of inner peace, being harmonious and without stress, is the easiest type of existence." ~ Norman Vincent Peale

Inner peace can mean many things to many people. You must decide what it will mean for you. What images come to mind when you think of inner peace in your own life? How would you feel if you were at peace? How would your life be different? What would you add to your routine and what would you take away? All of these questions need to be asked so the answers can be used as your personal tools to achieving the "calm."

The best explanation I've found is written in an article online that can be found at the following link: http://www.gotquestions.org/Bible-inner-peace.html.

There it gives a Biblical perspective on the word peace itself.

"A word often translated, "peace" in the Bible actually means 'to tie together as a whole, when all essential parts are joined together.' Inner peace, then, is a wholeness of mind and spirit, a whole heart at rest. Inner peace has little to do with external surroundings.

Jesus said, "Peace I leave with you; my peace I give you. I do not give to you as the world gives. Do not let your hearts be troubled and do not be afraid." He also told His followers that, 'in this world you will have many troubles. But take heart! I have overcome the world' (John 16:33). So peace is not the absence of trouble; it is the presence of God."

I believe Jesus wanted us to know that regardless of what happens in our lives, we must not seek inner peace beyond ourselves because if we do, we will never achieve it. There will always be something else to buy and someone else to be envious of. Something will always come along to blind side us and throw us off our game. Instead, if we integrate and trust in ourselves (and Him), nothing will be able to shake us. He is always with us, unlike any other person in our lives, and we carry Him inside of our soul. By accepting and integrating the changing tides and letting His plan unfold, we will know the peace He gave to us.

I believe peace is within all of us once we still our minds. I'm always on the go, when I settle for the night my thoughts are still racing making it difficult to quiet my mind so that I am completely restored. On my journey toward inner peace, I discovered that I control my mind and my thoughts and that made all the difference. I trusted in God's plan and trusted in the peace He promised could be mine. With the right tools you can too. I will elaborate more on these tools in later chapters but I want to mention some key components to my definition of inner peace.

Life must be lived with passion, desire and faith. We must be willing to stay in the present moment yet still be able to plan. When we plan, we must be able to adjust our plan without the wind leaving our sails or our world falling apart. We must be frugal with our time because it is something we can never get back. When we do give our time to someone or something, we must truly give it them, no half measures.

Journal Exercise – *Write down your definition of inner peace and what you think is stopping you from achieving it. Reflect on those things and begin to formulate a plan to remove thoughts and things from your life* *that don't serve you. Put down a thoughtful definition on paper on the first page of your journal that you can refer to often.*

Thoughts – *After you have written down your definition, spend some time researching what great thinkers have defined as inner peace. They can be religious leaders or philosophers or even people you have met in your own life who influenced you. We are all connected so it is ok to use the wisdom of those who have gone before us to help us navigate the path to inner peace.*

Plan – *When you have done your research and developed your definition, start to formulate an action plan that includes three things (no matter how small) you can do this week to take you one step closer to the definition you wrote on the first page of your journal.*

Chapter

What are the Obstacles?

"Do not let the behavior of others destroy your inner peace." ~Dalai Lama

Life doesn't always go the way we planned and for many of us, obstacles to inner peace exist in our own homes. Perhaps we are surrounded by family members who demand too much of our time and give nothing in return. Our home life can be draining. If we have children, the unconditional love they inspire goes hand in hand with the anxiety they cause. Many sleepless nights have been spent worrying about the fate of our children (especially if they are teenagers!). As our parents age, we worry about them as well and how best to care for them in their golden years. Running a household efficiently requires a multitude of skills and attention to detail.

Beyond the walls of our homes, many of us are actively involved in our communities. When we see things that aren't working in our church, or our business group, or our volunteer committee, or our town or our state, we can get caught up in trying to be a fixer. We over-invest our time and effort long after we should have moved on to the next thing. We cannot fix everyone's life or every town's problems. I am not suggesting that involvement in our communities is always negative, quite the opposite, being an involved citizen is vital to our growth and wellbeing. However, it goes back to being frugal with our time. We must be very thoughtful and ever mindful of where and to what our precious minutes and hours are devoted. If we aren't, this aspect of our lives can become an obstacle to finding peace.

For busy moms who work outside the home, the office can be a major obstacle to any kind of peace, especially inner peace. We face the demands of our job descriptions, the demands of bosses and co-workers, and the demands we place on ourselves to set and achieve career goals. If we have a job that we are passionate about, we are lucky. However, if that passion doesn't allow us to leave work at work, but instead to carry it with us everywhere we go, it has gone beyond the beneficial. The most detrimental work is work that inspires loathing instead of passion and work that leaves us feeling overworked, underpaid and underappreciated.

For many women, guilt is a constant companion. Even in 2016, women are made to feel that if they don't tow the line or stay within certain social boundaries, they should feel guilty about it. Guilt is a useless emotion, but society piles it on. Women are made to feel guilty if they work and guilty if they don't work. They are made to feel guilty if they are successful and guilty if they aren't. They are made to feel guilty about their looks, their clothes, their hair, their choice of mate, their choice of career, their choice of food and the choices their children make. Unfortunately, much of this guilt is passed on not only collectively by society but also from mother to daughter and so forth. For us to find inner peace, that cycle must be broken today. We must refuse to feel unnecessary guilt and we must refuse to pass it on to the next generation.

Alongside guilt are limiting beliefs that make women feel as though they can only reach a certain point. Fear then sets in and gives rise to more limiting beliefs. Examples such as, "I'll never be able to achieve that," "I always do that and it's so wrong," "I can't go any further," "I couldn't possibly ask for that, they'll just say no," "I'm not going to trust anyone again, I've been burned too many times" put a stranglehold on us and we stay stuck. These limiting beliefs affect our ideas of inner peace and it's achievability. We may think that the only people who can find inner peace are those who spend years alone in a cave navel gazing. If we set the limiting belief that inner peace is simply not a possibility in our hustle bustle world, we will follow a course that affirms that limiting belief. Limiting beliefs are dangerous. It may feel that stepping away from them is dangerous, but the opposite is true, clinging to them is even more dangerous.

All of these obstacles are very real components of our inner peace journey. We have to step beyond the demands of others at home and at work, step beyond our pointless guilt and limiting beliefs and commit to the process. Our commitment must be steadfast beginning with our personal definition of inner peace. We must define that calm and seek it out with every thought and action. I did it, and I know you can too.

Journal Exercise – *Observe what you say to yourself and what you say out loud to other people in the course of your life over the next few days. It can be during any interactions at all including family members, co-workers, friends, etc. In your journal write down a few scenarios you noticed that involve limiting beliefs. In what context did you express these limiting beliefs and where do you think you learned them? Write down any other obstacles you observe in your life that you feel may be hindering your quest for calm.*

Thoughts – *After you have reflected on the obstacles that may be stopping you from finding peace and the limiting beliefs you struggle with, spend some time reading inspirational stories about those people who have overcome obstacles and limiting beliefs and achieved life satisfaction.*

Plan – *For the next week, try to think before you speak a limiting belief and even think before you think a negative thought. If a limiting belief or negative thought does creep in, identify it, name it, figure out where it may have come from and counter it immediately either in your mind or on paper, with a positive thought and an empowering belief.*

Chapter 4

My Journey and New Ways of Living

"This is the day which the Lord hath made. We will be rejoice and be glad in it." ~ Psalms 118:24

I came to New York City with a box of vanilla wafer cookies, the clothes on my back and an idea that I would complete my studies at John Jay College of Criminal Justice. Being the first in my family to graduate high school, I didn't have any close role models. I just knew I wanted to do it.

It wasn't always smooth sailing. I had to work very hard to achieve my educational goals, all the while working to support my two children as a single mom. I cleaned rooms at the Red Roof Inn and fried chicken at Popeye's. I worked in retail, getting promoted from cashier to manager at a popular New York department store, Century 21. I worked as a teller at Manufacturer's Hanover Trust Bank until I finally got an opportunity that spearheaded my current job. I was appointed Community Liaison to the Project Manager in the Brooklyn District Attorney's Office. From there I continued my course working in public service as Deputy State Director to United States Senator Charles Schumer. Eventually I was given the position I hold today of Region II Advocate for the Small Business Administration for President Barack Obama's Administration. In my job I advocate on behalf of small businesses in New York, New Jersey, Puerto Rico and the U.S. Virgin Islands. I make sure their voices are heard when it comes to legislation that will affect them and their businesses. I love my job and I have found my inner peace. But I struggled.

When I first started in public service over twenty years ago, I didn't know how to pull back. I was determined to make the difference in the lives of whomever I came in contact with no matter what. Sleep was a luxury I couldn't afford at the time. If someone called me I had to answer. I had to respond to their need or their request right away. A colleague told me when I first started my career something that stuck with me in those early days: "The people you help may remember, the people you didn't help will never forget."

I made myself more than available. I never said no. I answered my phone 24 hours a day, 7 days a week for over six years. I felt like I had to be everything to everybody. The end result of this lifestyle had me feeling overwhelmed and unaccomplished. By being all things to all people, I had abandoned myself. I gained weight and lost my confidence. I knew I had to do something to feel good again, to feel whole again. I needed to find that calm space.

I started to pull back and honestly assess my situation. I started to prioritize my tasks but be realistic in my goals and in my daily life. I allowed myself to be a priority again. The most important thing I did was to say "no." The first time was hard but then it got easier. No is a word that stands on its own. You don't have to follow it with any kind of an explanation.

I used all the tools I am sharing with you in this guide. I learned to meditate and did it every day. I started keeping a journal. I did yoga and spent time with friends who built me up, instead of knocking me down. I pursued my dream to do motivational speaking. I knew if I gave myself a chance to do this, I would find a life I truly love and I was right. I know myself deep down and so do you. I got rid of what didn't serve me and focused my precious time on cultivating the life I now live.

Journal Exercise – *Write in your journal about your life journey and how you got to where you are today. What advantages did you have in your life? What disadvantages did you have? Are you a people pleaser and a "yes" person? Did a particular life event alter the course of your life? If so, what was it and how can you redirect?*

Thoughts – *After reflecting on your life and how your experiences shaped you, reflect on what you'd like your life story to be from this point on. Think about the life of someone you admire. They don't have to be famous or iconic, they can be someone you know. Did they have similar experiences to yours? What choices did they make that put them on the path they followed?*

Plan – *Write a new bio for yourself that you might give to someone who had never met you before and wanted to know who you are and what you stand for. Fill the bio with accomplishments that reflect your dreams and goals. Act as if these had already come true. Try to make the bio less than 500 words. This will encourage you to be compact in your thinking and really choose carefully what you want to include in your life story from this point on.*

Pathways to Inner Peace

"You will keep him in perfect peace, whose mind is stayed on You, because he trusts in You." ~ Isaiah 26:3

"Whatever the mind can conceive and believe, it can achieve." ~ Napoleon Hill

"I've learned that people will forget what you said, people will forget what you did, but people will never forget how you made them feel." ~ Maya Angelou

Remember, balance is a myth. New priorities will always interrupt. The scales cannot be in balance when you are experiencing the juggling act that is life. To achieve inner peace you have to think integration not balance. You must integrate the things into your life and schedule that help you realize your purpose. You will adjust as needed, and you will always be ready to adjust because you integrate, you don't seek "balance." Share your intentions (and your calendars!) with loved ones to keep them in the loop and to make sure that you include them in your integration. We have committed to taking care of ourselves, but no (wo)man is an island, we need to keep those near and dear to us in the loop. Isolation is not integration.

When I made my decision to change my life and seek inner peace, I knew I needed solid tools. I wanted a different life so I envisioned it. The first thing I did was to create a vision board and vision book of the life I wanted to have. I cut out pictures from magazines and put them in places I could see them. I repeated positive affirmations to myself throughout my days and I read scripture that empowered me and helped me remember that I am never alone. I also created a routine that included everything I mention below. These things are now part of daily life and they have helped me immeasurably. Make these tools habits, put them on the shared calendar, and integrate them into your life.

Meditation

When I wake up each morning, the first thing I do is meditate. It is a standing appointment I keep with myself. It is a way of starting my day off right. I have an attitude of gratitude because I have a fresh start and a chance to do my day right each morning. I adhere to my meditation as I would to any professional appointment because I am a priority. I know that if I don't do it, I will go back down the path of chaos and will lose my connection with the calm. I meditate because my health depends on it.

There is much mystery surrounding meditation. Many think you must sit in a candle lit room cross-legged for hours and if thoughts come into your head or you can't levitate, you did something wrong.

Nothing could be further from the truth. The goal of meditation is the quieting of the mind, but not the silencing of all thoughts. We are human. Thoughts will come into our heads. If we don't have thoughts, we are not living. The key is to acknowledge them but not dwell on them. Meditation can be done anywhere that feels safe and comfortable and there is no minimum or maximum time. I personally meditate for 15-20 minutes per day because that has worked for me, but everyone is different. If you can manage 15-20 minutes per day, I guarantee you will see results in your life that will assist in your inner peace journey.

A classic way of working toward stillness is to focus on the breath. You've heard this before because it works. The mere act of listening to your breath takes the focus away from the racing thoughts that threaten your inner peace. There are dozens of breathing exercises you can try that follow certain patterns that might appeal to you. For example, you can try holding you right nostril and breathing in through your left, then switching to your left nostril and breathing out through your right. You can also breathe in a numeric pattern. For instance, you can breathe in for four counts, hold for four counts, breathe out for four counts and hold for four counts. Another pattern you can follow is to breathe in for eight counts and breathe out in a long release. You can also breathe in for two and out for two, in rapid succession. These examples are just the tip of the iceberg. Some of them may feel comfortable for you and some you may find difficult or annoying. No problem, there will be many more for you to try until you find the pattern that complements your meditation session. I like to breathe in through my mouth and out through my nose while holding my hand on my belly and feeling the calm rise.

Some people have found that in addition to breathing, a mantra or prayer can be repeated over and over again to lure the mind away from chaotic thoughts. The mantra can be something as simple as the classic "ohm" repeated over and over again in conjunction with the breath, or even a holy name such as "Jesus," or "Yahweh." There is no right or wrong way to breathe, right or wrong thing to say or write or wrong length of time. The key is to be consistent and keep that meditation appointment each day. You owe it to yourself and life will reward you with more inner peace as a result. There are few guarantees in life, but if you give meditation a chance, I guarantee you will feel better about your situation.

Prayer

Like meditation, prayer is a very important part of my life and inner peace routine. At 5:00 a.m. each morning I have a prayer call with women throughout the United States. It helps me start my day with hope and pride. My prayer group and I study scripture and are thankful each day. We repent. We share our struggles, we pray for each other's family, finances, health, children, etc. It's a safe secure space with no judgment. We are able to honest and vulnerable. Prayer is another thing that rewards immeasurably. Peace and prayer go hand in hand.

Journaling

Throughout the chapters I have included a journaling exercise and I have done this because of the importance of writing your thoughts and beliefs on paper. When you journal, you begin to know yourself better by expressing your thoughts on paper instead of stewing about them in your mind. You begin to understand what it is you really want and what is holding you back. By journaling each day you have an accurate depiction of a particular event, and if the event is a happy one, you can go back to those memories and use them for your visualizations. If the memory is unpleasant, you can take solace in the fact that you released it and you never have to relive it. Your journaling can be a form of meditation or prayer itself and even if you don't think you have a single thing to write, go ahead and write that. It's ok if a journal entry begins with, "I have nothing to say." As you write that over and over you will find that soon other thoughts and feelings come flooding. Indeed you have a lot to say.

You can free-write to clear your mind and afterwards you can do some organized writing on specific things (examples: inspiration, prayer scriptures, family, career, wedding, exercise, health, buying a house, building wealth, running a successful business, marathon/triathlon, personal development, achieving inner peace). I write about all of these things in my journal. The hardest part about journaling is being consistent until the task is accomplished, but this is your journey and you must make yourself a priority.

Exercise and Diet Lead To Excellent Health

We cannot ignore our physical selves in our quest for inner peace, especially in this day and age. A culture of inactivity and unhealthy eating has created many problems for our population and it's up to us to say, "no more." Our bodies are worth taking care of and the better we treat them, the more time we will have to enjoy the inner peace we worked for. I make it a point to eat clean (lots of fruits and vegetables and little or no processed foods) and to move my body in some form of exercise. Nothing has to be taken to the extreme, but just like you will notice a difference in your life with consistent meditation and prayer, so too will you notice a difference in your health with clean eating and reasonable exercise. With food, I make it a point of not bringing things into my home that I know are not good for me. If they aren't there, I won't eat them!

My routine includes a workout from 6:00-7:00 five days a week. This time helps me blow-off steam and gets my adrenaline flowing. I attend classes at my local YMCA and use Groupon, Amazon, and other sites to get inexpensive classes to keep my workouts fresh and exciting (Shen Tao, Aqua Spin, Soul Cycle, belly dancing, Zumba, reggae, cross-fit, African dance, salsa, etc.). I even take my vision book with pictures to the gym and as I work out I focus on being healthy and strong.

Clutter free environment

In our consumer culture, there always seems to be a new temptation around the corner. Technology has worked wonders, there is no denying that, but I don't need to switch out my smart phone every year because the commercials tell me to! We have a tendency to accumulate too many material things and somehow equate success with "stuff". In a clutter-free environment, we have space to breathe, notice our breath and quiet our minds from the myriad distractions vying for our attention. A clutter-free environment and a purging of unnecessary things also helps our pocketbook. If we have money issues, and if we don't spend prudently and save, the constant stress of that existence will definitely create an obstacle to inner peace. If we stepped back and really thought about what we NEED in this world, we would be getting rid of a lot of what we HAVE that is simply unnecessary. Give yourself permission to create a clutter free environment, regardless of what the rest of the world thinks.

Like-Minded People, Loving and Harmonious Relationships

We know how important it is to surround ourselves with positive people, but despite this knowledge, there are still toxic people who remain in our lives. We can't seem to cut them loose. They may even be family members who are close to us and whom we've known all of our lives. It is a difficult task to remove someone from your life, but on your journey toward inner peace, it is a critical step. It doesn't need to include a knock down, drag out altercation. It can simply be a gradual distancing. When the life you create is drama free by design, you will begin to exude an energy that keeps toxic people at a distance. They will no longer seek you out because they feed off of an energy they can spot a mile away. If you don't exude that energy, they won't come and unload on you!

If you seek out like minded people to be around, you will find the task of removing toxic people from your life that much easier. There will be no time to cater to the drama or be saddled with the negativity. In your personal life and in your professional life, also seek out mentors. Some of us, myself included, had no immediately accessible role models. As an adult, I have overcome this by actively seeking the company of those who inspire me and seeking out mentors to put me on the path to success. This has paid off for me. I have a rewarding career for which I have worked hard. I love what I do and I love helping people. It's my life's purpose and in order to do it most effectively, I must work on achieving peace.

In my personal life I still have a tendency to be a fixer so I am often called to do things that my family members could and should do for themselves. Maybe you are in the same position in your family. Along the way on this journey, I have stopped doing everything for everyone at the expense of myself. Instead I have chosen to give guidance without taking on everyone's problems. I still nurture my relationships and make everyone feel important with special time and attention, but not at the expense of taking care of myself. When I begin to feel depleted, I take "me" time and step away. I go back to these inner peace tools and find that calm again.

Journal Exercise - *What are some of the things that keep you up at night? Write them down and compare them to the list of limiting beliefs you did in the earlier exercise. Do you find yourself dwelling on things that you cannot change or control? What would your life be like if you were able to let go of these thoughts or ideas? Now write down things that make you smile and make a point of visualizing them.*

Thoughts – *Have you made yourself a priority today? Have you been kind to yourself and repeated positive affirmations? Have you kept your appointment with meditation today? Have you eaten clean and moved your body?*

Plans – *Create a vision board of the things you thought about that made you smile. Take great care in completing this vision board and put it somewhere where you will always see it and can refer to it easily. Make a point of looking at it before your meditation session if you can. These tangible reminders of what makes you smile will immediately change your neurobiology when you look at them.*

Chapter 6

More Tools for Inner Peace

"Peace I leave with you, My peace I give to you; not as the world gives do I give to you. Let not your heart be troubled, neither let it be afraid." ~ John 14:27

"These things I have spoken to you, that in Me you may have peace. In the world you will have tribulation; but be of good cheer, I have overcome the world." ~ John 16:33

"Be anxious for nothing, but in everything by prayer and supplication, with thanksgiving, let your requests

be made known to God; and the peace of God, which
surpasses all understanding, will guard your hearts and
minds through Christ Jesus." ~ Philippians 4:6-7

In the Bible, Jesus tells us clearly that peace is possible for us if
we look to the peace He left for us, not look to this world and its
temptations. If we look to the world, we will always be disappointed. If
we look to Him, we will always be satisfied.

As children, we are filled with wonder and joy. We believe in
miracles. In fact, we will believe anything anyone tells us. We are
innocent. As we grow older and become more jaded, have our hearts
broken and experience hardship, we lose our sense of wonder and we
replace it with fear and bitterness. Sometimes we turn to addictive
substances to help us forget our troubles, quickly learning that those
substances take us down a wretched path with lightening speed. Other
times we decide to fill our lives with material goods, thinking a certain
lifestyle will bring back our joy and wonder. Again, we are disappointed.
We step onto life's treadmill and we feel like we can't get off. Our self
worth becomes tied to what others think of us or to our success instead
of remembering that we are still God's children, filled with wonder and
joy. Miracles still happen, we've just stopped seeing them. What we are
seeking never left. It was always there, we just turned our collective
back on it.

On my inner peace journey, I turned to God and to prayer as a
critical component to rediscovering wonder, joy and peace in my life.
Because of my faith and religious tradition, it was a natural path for me
to find Him in that calm space. Not everyone is raised in a religious
tradition or is a Christian. But that doesn't mean that prayer can't
be a part of the journey. You don't have to read the Bible. There are
many spiritual texts that can help you on the path. You just need to

find the one that is right for you. If you do turn to the Bible, you will discover God's peace on nearly every page. Scripture can be part of your meditation process, your mentoring process or your vision book. It can be the intention you set at the beginning of each yoga class. It can fill the pages of your journal. True wisdom doesn't make us cynical. It makes us wonder-ful. The Bible is filled with wisdom.

I pray daily, beginning with my prayer call each morning and I have found that Jesus is central to my journey. Indeed, he is called the Prince of Peace (Isaiah 9:6). He IS peace. When no one else is there to help and guide, He is there. He fills the universe with his loving energy. We just need to turn our hearts and minds to him, even if it's just for a few minutes each day. Soon we will find Him in everything and see His love everywhere we turn. Of all the tools I have used on my quest for inner peace, my relationship with God has been the touchstone.

Journal Exercise – *If you come from a religious background, but have wandered away from it, spend some time reflecting on what it meant to you*

as you were growing up and write about that in your journal. What part did religion play in your life? How does your belief system influence your life and choices even if you haven't been actively involved in it for weeks, months or even years? Do you ever long to get involved again? Have you thought about seeking out others to guide you on your faith journey?

Thoughts – *What would your life look like now if religion still played a role? How can you incorporate religious tradition and prayer into your life given your current circumstances? Would it be easy or difficult? Would you find support from friends and family or would you be met with resistance and skepticism?*

Plan – *Spend some time exploring theology and spirituality by reading some of the great religious writers. You can read from the Bible, you can read from the Tao or you can do some research and find out what spiritual traditions might appeal to you. When you have found some philosophies that seem to fit what you are looking for, make a plan to incorporate them slowly into your life and inner peace journey. Go to a service, find a mentor, keep studying. Reassess every three months and see how spirituality has enhanced your inner peace journey.*

Chapter

What is Life Like In The Calm Space?

"Your heart knows the way. Run in that direction." ~Rumi

By following the exercises and suggestions I outline in this guide, a new way of life will emerge for you. It's a way of life that includes inner peace. Now, I can spend quality time in the calm space and I have everything I want and need. I have passion and desire in my life and work. My faith is strong. I plan but I am flexible. I integrate my life and am frugal with my time. When I do give my time, I give it wholeheartedly and joyfully.

Not every day is perfect and life throws us curveballs. But because I live an integrated and mindful life that is based in faith and love, I can accept life's curveballs and integrate them appropriately. If something comes up that is out of my control and causes needless worry, I am able to meditate on it and let it go. I can look to the Bible and reach out to my prayer circle or a trusted mentor. If something transpires that requires action, I can prioritize appropriately without becoming frazzled or putting counter productive pressure on myself to deal with it. After integrating, I can return to my routine and re-establish my equilibrium. I can quickly go back to the calm space and rest there.

We all have the same 24-hour day. But because I choose to make myself a priority and choose to seek out joy and peace in my life, I am spared the constant turmoil of an existence that is out of control. I choose to make a path that will lead to heart-centered calm. I choose to have confidence in the process, in God and to understand that bliss is just on the other side of chaos. It's within reach. Each day I choose to use all the tools that are available to me. And the best part is, they are free of charge.

You too can achieve inner peace in your daily life by incorporating integration and using the tools that I have outlined for you. I urge you to try them all and give the process your full commitment. I promise you won't be disappointed. Instead, you'll be at peace. And that is my sincere wish for you.

Chapter

A Life of Inner Peace

"When there is no enemy within, the enemies outside cannot hurt you." ~African Proverb

Have you ever met someone whose positive energy you could immediately feel? Have you ever been drawn to someone inexplicably? Have you ever been in a situation where there was chaos all around and there was someone completely at ease amid the chaos? That is what a life of inner peace looks like. There is no enemy within, so the "enemies" without, fear, anxiety, judgment, self-loathing, anger, cannot make a dent. The opposite is true when you meet someone whose negative energy is palpable and makes you want to run for the hills!

A life of inner peace doesn't mean a life without hardship. It just means that the inner peace that has been cultivated through the tools described: meditation, yoga, journaling, vision boards, prayer, exercise and clean eating, has fortified you to the point where you simply don't react the same when something doesn't go the way you planned.

A life of inner peace is a life of total gratitude for each moment lived. It is a life filled with self-acceptance and self-love as well as love for others and a complete lack of judgment. It is a life without fear filled with a lot of smiles and genuine enjoyment. Soon you will be the person that everyone is drawn to in a crowded room. They will ask you what your secret is and how you are so calm, so happy and so peaceful.

Can you imagine a world where everyone was on a committed pathway to inner peace? It would be a world of acceptance and understanding instead of a world of judgment and conflict.

It cannot be reiterated enough that if you choose to work on yourself and find that calm space, you will be able to give your true self to every aspect of your life, instead of presenting the fear based false self to the world. Your life will be truly blessed.

A life of inner peace will make your dreams a reality because your head will be clear enough and your heart will be ready to accept exactly what it is you were meant to do and achieve. If you give in to the constant chatter in your minds, you become paralyzed with fear and self-doubt. Inner peace removes those destructive thought processes and replaces them with joy, bliss and BELIEF.

So make yourself a priority starting right now. Get your journal going, start your vision board, spend a few minutes meditating, sign up for a yoga class, say a prayer of thanksgiving, say something nice to yourself and really mean it. A life of inner peace is waiting for you. It's within your reach and you deserve it. Enjoy the journey and God bless you.

Printed and bound by PG in the USA

USA2019PGIL